Myth or Reality?

What it means to be gifted...
and what it doesn't!

Myth or Reality?
What it means to be gifted...
and what it doesn't!

Patricia Farrenkopf, Ed.D

Owner and Creator of

PGi TM
ProGift-ify

Fishtail Publishing

Book design by Erin O'Neil
www.erinoneil.org

Cover design by Erin O'Neil

Fishtail Publishing
Published in the USA by Fishtail Publishing LLC
Westerville, OH

www.fishtailpublishing.org

ISBN: 978-1-7333380-5-9
Library of Congress Control Number: 2020923724

This book is dedicated to all of the gifted individuals who are more different from each other than they are alike. Delightful! May you always be YOU and be able to count on advocates (and become your own advocate) to continue to correct the myths - to change myths into reality.

Table of Contents

Introduction 1

Myth vs. Reality - Which is It? 7

A Declaration of the Rights of a Gifted Child 40

Bill of Rights for the Gifted 44

Bill of Rights for Teachers 45

Bill of Rights for Parents 46

Card Games

Sorting Myths from Realities 48

A Match! Myth with its Reality 49

Appendix A – Gifted Brain Differences 50

Appendix B – Gifted Characteristics and Resulting Behaviors 53

Reference List 59

Acknowledgments

My mentors in education and gifted...

the late Elizabeth McKethan
the late Dr. Raymond Swassing
Penny Guy

"If you tell the truth, you don't have to remember anything."

Mark Twain

Introduction

I have been learning about, working with, and teaching educators about gifted and high ability learners for most of my career in education. An area of interest I have always had, but did not have a name for until I was well into my teaching career, was the misunderstandings many children and adults had about being gifted.

In 1973, I started my teaching career in a rural school district in eastern North Carolina. My 38 fifth graders included children with a range of abilities - from those who were not yet reading beyond a second grade level, all the way to those who were performing well above grade level expectations. The vast majority of the children were average in ability and achieving quite nicely at grade level. Similar to my teaching colleagues at the time, I designed instruction for the large percentage of children who were achieving at grade level. Most of us did not adequately address the needs of either end of the spectrum - the struggling students and the ones who were advanced were not served.

The advantages that came with the October 4, 1957 launching of the Russian Sputnik satellite and the resulting U.S. concentration on advanced math and science education were well in the past. We had successfully sent men into orbit, so the space race crisis was over. There was no longer the sense of urgency to grow our potential mathematicians and scientists. There was certainly not recognition of a need to assist our academically and physically challenged students until a few years after my entry into the teaching profession.

Then, in 1975, Congress enacted PL 94-142, the Education for All Handicapped Children Act (IDEA). The purpose of this law was to ensure educational rights for our handicapped students, to meet their individual needs, and to improve the level of achievement experienced by these learners. For 42 years, this legislation has provided a national and state by state focus on providing an appropriate education for these children. Early identification and services for preschool-age children and public school special education strive to provide 6 million students with the least restrictive environment for education in their own neighborhoods and schools (US Department of Education, 2007.) All children with disabilities receive a free and appropriate education designed to meet their unique needs. The rights of children with disabilities and their parents are protected. State and local districts receive federal assistance. Assessment of effectiveness of special education programs has also always been a part of the law.

Once this law was enacted, I worked with a newly hired special education teacher who met with the identified special education students for academic instruction. I had these children in my classroom only for homeroom and the special area classes of art, music, and physical education. Our staff took a college level credit-bearing course on the education of handicapped students with the cost covered by our district and offered at our school location after school hours. In my undergraduate training in the late 1960s and early 1970s, I was not presented with concepts for meeting the needs of special education students. I was very happy to have this course offered.

Although I still had the students who were above grade level, I predictably continued to teach to the middle. I naively thought that a law mandating the service for our advanced students would be forthcoming. I was wrong and have been waiting for the same 42 years over which time the IDEA has been growing and refining. I completed an M.A.Ed. in 1984 with a concentration in gifted education. In my career, I have taught and coordinated gifted services, served as a principal, and retired from administration. I soon returned to the role of a gifted services coordinator in order to continue my advocacy for this underserved population.

In 2018, the Gifted Operating Standards in Ohio were revised. Lawmakers finally recognized that general education teachers do not have any gifted education courses in their repertoire, yet are still expected to meet the needs of gifted students in their classrooms. As Gottfredson (2003) has pointed out, "Gifted students are just as statistically significantly different from average as is the other end of the spectrum." Knowledge of nature and needs as well as curriculum and instruction of and for gifted learners are critical skill sets that our educators need to possess in order to appropriately teach these students. The new operating standards also address the need to consider underrepresented populations, such as those who are twice exceptional. Twice exceptional individuals will benefit from this section, shedding light on the fact that you can be both gifted and learning disabled.

A continual issue to confront is the many myths believed about gifted individuals...children and adults alike. I was first formally made aware of these myths and truths through The Jacob Javits Gifted and Talented Students Education Act. This Act, also known as Javits, was first passed by Congress in 1988 as part of the Elementary and Secondary Education Act, and was most recently reauthorized through the Every Student Succeeds Act to support the development of talent in U.S. schools. The Javits Act, which is the only federal program dedicated specifically to gifted and talented students, does not fund local gifted education programs. The purpose of the Jacob Javits Gifted and Talented Students Education Act is to orchestrate a coordinated program of scientifically based research, demonstration projects, innovative strategies, and similar activities that build and enhance the ability of elementary and secondary schools to meet the special educational needs of gifted and talented students.

The Javits Act focuses resources on identifying and serving students who are traditionally underrepresented in gifted and talented programs, particularly minority, economically disadvantaged, English language learners, and students with disabilities, to help reduce gaps in achievement and to encourage the establishment of equal educational opportunities for all students. In addition to the demonstration grants, the Javits program funds a National Research and Development Center for the Education of Gifted and Talented Children and Youth, which conducts a focused program of research that includes an exploratory study, an impact evaluation, and leadership and outreach activities to ensure that the research informs education practice. The Javits program, like other authorized federal grant programs, must be funded each year by the Congress.

So, that is the background of Myths and Realities of Gifted. Now, let's look at some of those myths and a deeper explanation of why they are believed, but also why they are not true. Also, let's consider some educational tools that will assist the parents and teachers who work and guide gifted students to be well versed in the myths ...and most of all, the realities!

~ Patricia Farrenkopf ~

"It is only with the heart
that one can see rightly;
what is essential is invisible to the eye."

Antoine de Saint-Exupery

"All you have to do is write
one true sentence.
Write the truest sentence that you know."

Ernest Hemingway

Which Is It?

On the following pages, you will consider statements on the page on the right and decide whether you think they are myths or realities.

Then, after turning to the next page, the page on the left will not only reveal whether the statement is a myth or a reality...but it will also provide an explanation.

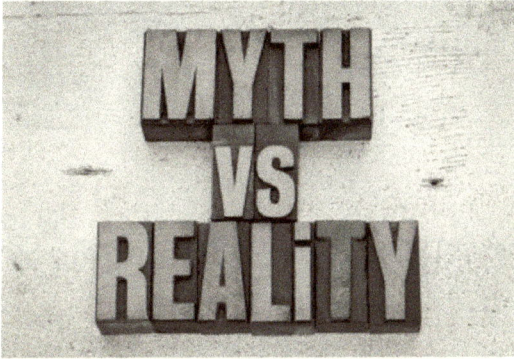

There are over 180 different definitions of giftedness.

Turn the page to find out if it is a myth or reality

REALITY

There are over 180 different definitions of giftedness.

This is a reality.

A definition is *a statement of an exact meaning of a word, especially in a dictionary.* How could there be so many different definitions of giftedness?

Defining the term gifted is no easy task. Numerous definitions have been suggested, but no single definition of giftedness is accepted by everyone or even by a majority of people. Because so many definitions exist, people often get confused over just what it means to be gifted.

Not only that, parents and teachers sometimes find it difficult to communicate, because what they say is based on different definitions!

Gifted children don't need help.
They will do fine on their own.

Turn the page to find out if it is a myth or reality

Gifted children don't need help.
They will do fine on their own.

This is a myth.

In a typical classroom, there can be students from one end of the spectrum to the other. When resources are limited, it is often believed that any available resources should be focused on those children who absolutely positively cannot make it without much assistance. Those children may include the economically disadvantaged, the mentally and physically handicapped, the bilingual, and other groups singled out for support beyond normal funding levels.

Gifted students need guidance from well-trained teachers who challenge and support them in order to fully develop their abilities. Many gifted students may be so far ahead of their same-age peers that they know more than half of the grade-level curriculum before the school year begins. Their resulting boredom and frustration can lead to low achievement, despondency, or unhealthy work habits.

The role of the teacher is crucial for spotting and nurturing talents in school. Think about it - we would never send a star athlete to train for the Olympics without a coach.

Gifted students make everyone else in the class smarter by providing a role model or tutor.

Turn the page to find out if it is a myth or reality

Gifted students make everyone else in the class smarter by providing a role model or tutor.

This is a myth.

Many gifted students spend most, if not all of their time in school in mixed ability classrooms. If it is true that many gifted students may be so far ahead of their same-age peers that they know more than half of the grade level curriculum before the school year begins, it might make sense that they could help the teacher by being a tutor for those children who are having difficulty learning that same curriculum.

It is a positive to establish a classroom community that is empathetic to all. Average or below-average students do not look to the gifted students in the class as role models. Watching or relying on someone who is expected to succeed does little to increase a struggling student's sense of self-confidence.

Gifted students need to be with others of similar ability for at least part of their school experience. They are also attending school with the expectation they will receive an appropriate experience. There are many other opportunities for all children to learn empathy and be helpful to one another.

We can find all of our gifted by using approved
ability and achievement tests.

Turn the page to find out if it is a myth or reality

We can find all of our gifted by using approved ability and achievement tests.

This is a myth.

Ability and achievement test results provide numbers or scores to demonstrate a child's performance in comparison to others. Tests provide a variety of scores, including raw scores, percentile ranks, grade-equivalent scores, and standard scores. Assessments must be current (recent norms). Typically, tests for identification are approved at the state level. However, test norms should reflect the local demographic, not only national norms.

Formal assessments are only one tool in determining giftedness. Tests should be used in conjunction with subjective assessment tools. In identifying creative thinkers and visual and performing arts talents, checklists are an integral part of the identification process. It is important to review sub scores, as twice-exceptional students can be overlooked if only using a general score.

It is also important to remember that some students can be gifted in one area and disabled in another. They need to be identified and served for both.

The intellectual ability level of gifted is at the same level as their social and emotional development.

Turn the page to find out if it is a myth or reality

The intellectual ability level of gifted is at the same level as their social and emotional development.

This is a myth.

Gifted students are often intellectually ahead of their age placement in school. They often seek out company with older students so they can converse about topics in which they have a passion and advanced understanding. Many times, their intellectual understanding of topics has been developed through an intense interest and resulting research outside of the school day.

There are many examples of gifted students achieving recognition in invention and problem solving and they have made a significant difference in our world. Asynchronous development of gifted students means that their intellectual level is different from that of their social and emotional development. The more gifted the child, the more asynchronous that child may be.

There can be drastic differences between a gifted child's physical, intellectual, social, and emotional development. A gifted child can have the intelligence of an adult with the social-emotional development of a child. It is often said that gifted children are "many ages at once."

Gifted students are more different from each other than they are alike.

Turn the page to find out if it is a myth or reality

REALITY

Gifted students are more different from each other than they are alike.

This is a reality.

Areas of Giftedness include: cognitive, specific academic, creative, visual and performing arts, leadership, and psychomotor.

Common Characteristics of Gifted include:
- Early talkers with precise vocabularies
- Ability to quickly process information
- High curiosity level
- High memory retention
- Intense in the way they learn
- Exhibit well-developed sense of humor
- Acute sense of justice
- Strong imagination
- Keen observation
- Effective problem solving skills

Because gifted children are so diverse, not all exhibit all characteristics. Even those who exhibit most of the characteristics do not exhibit them all of the time or in every area. In addition, gifted individuals can be gifted in one or more of the following areas:
- General intellectual ability
- Specific academic ability
- Creative thinking ability
- Visual/performing arts
- Leadership
- Psychomotor (sports as one example)

Gifted students need to be taught studying and test taking skills.

Turn the page to find out if it is a myth or reality

REALITY

Gifted students need to be taught studying and test taking skills.

This is a reality.

Many gifted students come to school already knowing how to read and how to solve simple math problems. Gifted students often are so advanced that they know most of the content of their grade / age level placement before they even start the school year. Gifted students are often able to memorize facts quickly and find much of what is expected of them in school really easy. They really seem to succeed effortlessly.

Many gifted students do not really experience true academic challenge until they are in high school - or even college. Education often requires memorization and then repeating those facts in their own words on a project or at a later date on a test. When these students encounter the more rigorous and demanding curriculum, if they have not learned studying or test taking skills, they may be without the effective habits necessary when their work requires more application of concepts rather than just memorization of facts.

Gifted students can be very perfectionistic and may need assistance in taking risks.

Turn the page to find out if it is a myth or reality

REALITY

Gifted students can be very perfectionistic and may need assistance in taking risks.

This is a reality.

Being perfect is often seen as:

- Being possible with hard work
- Within reach if you always do your best
- The way to be successful
- Always working for positive outcomes
- Always being a leader
- Making it possible to be confident
- A strength
- Something you will always be

In reality, gifted students may find it very difficult to take risks. Perfection isn't possible; it isn't real, and this makes perfectionism a real problem for many people. None of us is or ever will be perfect or without faults. Gifted students need to have support to take risks and, yes, even fail when taking those risks. Finding books about how individuals have used failure to find success is a good way to help gifted students understand that failure is part of life and can lead to understanding.

Gifted students who are sequential learners can get lost when there are multiple steps.

Turn the page to find out if it is a myth or reality

REALITY

Gifted students who are sequential learners can get lost when there are multiple steps.

This is a reality.

A sequential learner...
- May be more likely to respond to a problem with logic first, instead of emotion.
- May feel the need to understand each part of an equation.
- May be good with time management, and probably gets to school on time.
- May tend to remember names.
- May have notes that are divided and labeled. They may categorize things a lot.
- May feel most comfortable when planning ahead.

What is the challenge of being a sequential learner?
- You may fall in love with the details when reading. You have to understand something before you move on.
- You might get frustrated easily with people who don't understand things as quickly as you do.

What can help?
- Seeing a short overview before jumping into the details
- Connecting the specific details to the larger concepts

Gifted students who are spatial learners may not be able to explain how they got their answers.

Turn the page to find out if it is a myth or reality

REALITY

Gifted students who are spatial learners may not be able to explain how they got their answers.

This is a reality.

A spatial learner...
- May be more likely to respond to a problem with emotion first, instead of logic.
- Can accept an equation without understanding how it works.
- May be late for school a lot because they are constantly thinking.
- Tends to remember faces, but forget names.
- May act on impulse
- Might be just fine about playing music while studying. (Some students can't concentrate while music plays.)
- Might not raise their hand much to answer questions because it takes a while to sort out your answer.
- When they eventually do come up with an answer, it is much more thorough.
- Are likely to read and read and become frustrated, and then suddenly "get it."

What is the challenge of being a spatial learner?
- You tend to pass over the small details to pursue the big idea
- You can spend so much time thinking that is difficult to react to a question that requires an instant answer.

What can help?
- Outlines for new material
- See the steps that lead to the big idea

The Brain...
When you learn something new, your brain becomes more wrinkled.

Turn the page to find out if it is a myth or reality

The Brain...
When you learn something new, your brain becomes more wrinkled.

This is a myth.

Our brain has ridges and crevices. These ridges and crevices are often referred to as wrinkles of the brain. The ridges are called **gyri** and the crevices are called **sulci**.

The brain has become larger over time to accommodate all of the higher functions that set us apart from other animals. In order to keep the brain compact enough to fit into a skull that would actually be in proportion with the rest of our body size, the brain folded in on itself as it grew. If we unfolded all of those ridges and crevices, the brain would be the size of a pillowcase.

The gyri and sulci we're born with are the wrinkles we have for life, assuming that our brains remain healthy. Our brains do change when we learn -- it's just not in the form of additional sulci and gyri. This growth is called **brain plasticity**.

By studying changes in the brains of animals like rats as they learn tasks, researchers have discovered that **synapses** (the connections between neurons) and the blood cells that support neurons is what actually grows and increases in number. Some believe that we get new neurons when we make new memories, but this hasn't yet been proven in human brains.

The human brain is the biggest brain.

Turn the page to find out if it is a myth or reality

The human brain is the biggest brain.

This is a myth.

Many animals can use their brains to do some of the things that humans can do, such as:

- Finding creative ways to solve problems
- Exhibiting awareness of self
- Demonstrating empathy toward others
- Learning how to use tools in a purposeful way

There is general agreement that humans are the most intelligent creatures on Earth. We also know that our brains change as we learn. The average adult human brain weighs about 3 pounds.

The dolphin, a very intelligent animal, also has a brain that weighs about 3 pounds on average. But a sperm whale, not considered to be as intelligent as a dolphin, has a brain that weighs about 17 pounds. The brain of a beagle is about 2.5 ounces, and the weight of an orangutan brain is about 13 ounces.

Both dogs and orangutans are pretty smart animals, but they have small brains. The relationship between brain size and intelligence isn't really about the actual weight of the brain; it's about the ratio of brain weight to the entire body weight.

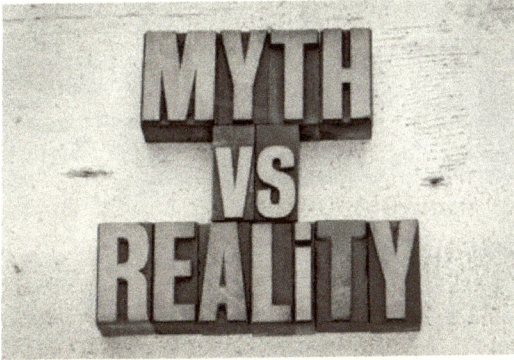

We only use 10 % of our brain.

Turn the page to find out if it is a myth or reality

We only use 10 % of our brain.

This is a myth.

American psychologist of the early 1900s, William James, said that the average person rarely achieves but a small portion of his or her potential. Professor William James of Harvard said that the average man develops only ten percent of his latent mental ability.

We can become disabled from damage to just a small area of the brain depending on location, so there is absolutely no way that we could function with only 10 percent of our brain. Brain scans have shown that, no matter what we are doing, our brains are always active. Some areas are more active at any one time than others, but unless we have brain damage, there is no one part of the brain that is absolutely not functioning.

Here's an example. If you're sitting at a table and eating a sandwich, you're not actively using your feet. You're concentrating on bringing the sandwich to your mouth, chewing and swallowing it. But that doesn't mean that your feet aren't working -- there's still activity in them even when you're not actively moving them.

If you are gifted in one area, that makes up for not being gifted - or even having a learning challenge - in another area.

Turn the page to find out if it is a myth or reality

If you are gifted in one area, that makes up for not being gifted - or even having a learning challenge - in another area.

This is a myth.

All individuals have strengths and weaknesses. These strengths and weaknesses are experienced at different levels. Gifted areas listed by the National Association for Gifted Children list the following 6 areas of giftedness: *Intellectual, Academic Achievement, Creative Thinking, the Arts, Leadership, and Psychomotor.*

Individuals with Disabilities Education Act list 13 areas of special education including Autism, Specific Learning Disabilities and Handicapping Disabilities and Impairments. In each of the areas, the degree of gifted or special education required depends upon the unique needs of the individual.

In a 2011 study by the Office of Special Education Programs, more than 1.5 million children identified for special education services may very well meet the criteria to also be identified as gifted. These individuals are exceptional in two ways - or twice exceptional.

A vast majority of gifted students are not gifted in all areas and it is the same for students with disabilities...they are not disabled in all areas. Both of these exceptionalities need to be addressed in order for students to thrive academically, socially, and emotionally. Using student strengths to addresses areas of need is a very vital part of the education of all, including our twice exceptional students.

Twice exceptional students can have both an IEP and a WEP.

Turn the page to find out if it is a myth or reality

REALITY

Twice exceptional students can have both an IEP and a WEP.

This is a reality.

An IEP (Individualized Education Plan) is a plan or program developed to ensure that a child who has a disability identified under the law, and is attending an elementary or secondary educational institution, receives specialized instruction and related services.

A WEP (Written Education Plan) is a plan or program developed to ensure that a child who is gifted under the law, and attending an elementary or secondary educational institution, receives instruction based on the individual's needs.

Their plans should include...

- Teaching strategies that compensate for their areas of need while introducing challenges in their areas of strength
- Teaching strategies that will help them overcome weaknesses, rather than asking the student to "try harder"
- Delivering materials in the way they learn the best
- Trying different methods until you find the right fit
- Focusing on strengths to remediate weaknesses
- Providing appropriate pacing; faster in areas of strength and more time in areas of weakness

In a democracy, Jefferson once said when referring to equal,

"There is nothing more unequal than equal treatment of unequal people."

Every child is unique.

All children have a right to develop their own potential.

All children must include gifted children.

A Declaration of the Educational Rights of the Gifted Child

Barbara Clark, Ed.D.

A Declaration of the Educational Rights of the Gifted Child

1. It is the right of a gifted child to engage in appropriate educational experiences even when other children of the grade level or age are not following the same path.

2. It is the right of a gifted child to be grouped and to interact with other gifted children for some part of the learning experience in order to be understood, engaged, and challenged.

3. It is the right of a gifted child to be taught rather than be used as a tutor or teaching assistant for the major part of the school day.

4. It is the right of a gifted child to be presented with new, advanced, and challenging ideas and concepts regardless of the materials and resources that have been designated for the age group or grade level in which the child was placed.

5. It is the right of a gifted child to be taught the concepts that the child does not yet know instead of relearning old concepts that the child has already shown evidence of mastering.

6. It is the right of a gifted child to learn faster than age peers and to have that pace of learning respected and provided for.

7. It is the right of a gifted child to think in alternative ways, produce diverse products, and to bring intuition and innovation to the learning experience.

8. It is the right of a gifted child to be idealistic and sensitive to fairness, justice, accuracy, and the global problems facing humankind and to have a forum for expressing these concerns.

9. It is the right of a gifted child to question generalizations, offer alternative solutions, and value complex and profound levels of thought.

10. It is the right of a gifted child to be intense, persistent, and goal-directed in the pursuit of knowledge.

11. It is the right of a gifted child to express a sense of humor that is unusual, playful, and often complex.

12. It is the right of a gifted child to hold high expectations for self and others and to be sensitive to inconsistency between ideals and behavior; the child may need to have help in seeing the value in human differences.

13. It is the right of a gifted child to be a high achiever in some areas of the curriculum and not in others making thoughtful, knowledgeable academic placement a necessity.

14. It is the right of a gifted child to have a low tolerance for the lag between vision and actualization, between personal standards and developed skill, and between physical maturity and athletic ability.

15. It is the right of a gifted child to pursue interests that are beyond the ability of age peers, are outside of the grade level curriculum, or involve areas as yet unexplored or unknown.

These are some of the rights of gifted children for which we must advocate. From your experience you will probably wish to add more, but if we could only be sure that the educational experiences of the gifted children we serve honored these 15 rights we would have the assurance that our society would be blessed with a continuous supply of gifted adults. We would be sure we had nurtured the gifted children among us.

Barbara Clark, Ed.D.

You Have a Right to...

• Know about your giftedness.

• Learn something new everyday.

• Be passionate about your talent area without apologies.

Gifted Children's Bill of Rights

• Have an identity beyond your talent area.

National Association for Gifted Children

• Feel good about your accomplishments.

• Make mistakes.

• Seek guidance in the development of your talent.

Del Siegle

• Have multiple peer groups and a variety of friends.

• Choose which of your talent areas you wish to pursue.

• Not to be gifted at everything.

Teachers of Gifted Students Have a Right to...

Bill of Rights for Teachers of Gifted Students

National Association for Gifted Children

Del Siegle

• Advocate for their students and their best interests.

• Modify the existing curriculum.

• Attend comprehensive training to aid in identifying and serving gifted children from all backgrounds.

• Seek out new and innovative ideas and resources.

• Try new approaches, strategies, practices, and tools in the classroom.

• Provide enrichment opportunities driven by student interest and passion.

• Promote the skills of higher order thinking, problem solving, creativity, and autonomous learning.

• Supportive state and district policies for gifted programs and services.

• Take into account their students' diverse social, emotional, cultural, and economic backgrounds.

• Set the standard for great educational practice.

• Say, "This student needs something different."

**Bill of Rights
for Parents of
Gifted Children**

**Gifted
Guru**

Lisa Van Gemert

Parents of Gifted Children Have a Right to...

- Patience and understanding on the part of friends, family, and educators with the unique parenting required for raising gifted children.

- Not be accused of bragging when you share your child's achievements because it doesn't always come easily, even to the gifted.

- Get support in the educational setting for your child's needs, even if the child is passing the state tests.

- Have your child's exceptionalities accurately diagnosed and served.

- Educational and mental health professionals who understand and are effectively trained in giftedness.

- Not be the only person who is determined to make sure your child has the time & materials to explore his or her gifts fully.

- Choose the best educational environment for your child without judgment from others, even if the best environment is home.

- Expect your child to be physically, emotionally, and cognitively safe at school and social situations.

- Allow your child to not always have to be successful.

- Celebrate your child's gifts without apology, hesitation, or fear.

"Truth is ever to be found in simplicity,
and not in the multiplicity and confusion of things."

Sir Isaac Newton

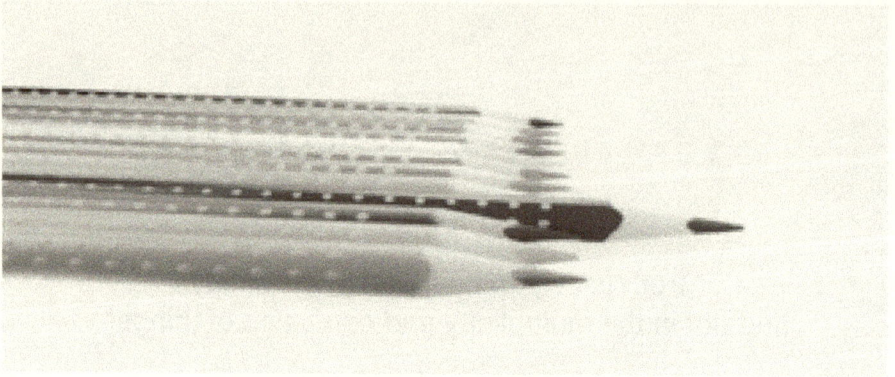

Sorting Myths from Realities
A Card Game

Shuffle the deck of cards.

Deal all of the cards to the players.

Player one lays one of their cards face up. The person who has the opposite of that card adds their card to the one face up and takes that sort for their count.

The game continues until all cards have been sorted and collected.

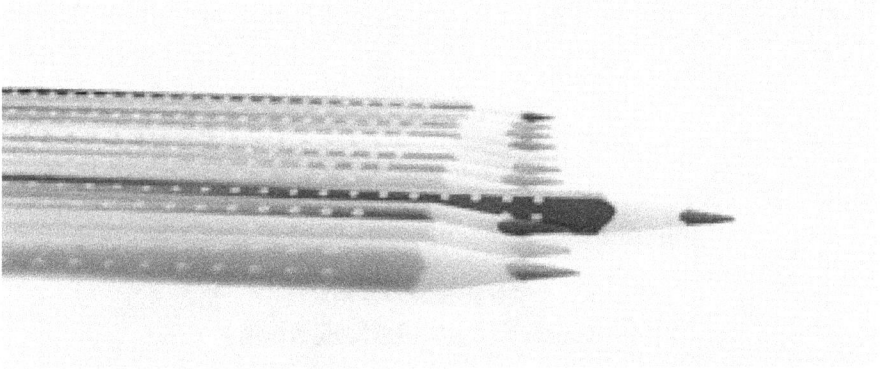

A Match!
Myth with its Reality
A Card Game

Take all of the reality red suit cards (hearts and diamonds) and lay them face down in front of the players.

Shuffle the remaining myth black suit cards (clubs and spades) and deal to the players.

Each player gets 3 cards. The remaining black cards are placed face down in a stack, with the first card turned up.

The first player turns over the top red suit card. They can then either take the black suit card that is face up or draw a card. If they have a red card that is opposite of a black card, they play that match in front of them. That player then discards one of their black myth cards.

The game continues until a player has played all of their cards and discarded the last one in their hand.

Appendix A
Gifted Brain Differences

M | Morphology
That means size, quantity, shape of brain anatomy

O | Operations
That means neural efficiency and speed of connections in the brain

R | Real Estate
That means the differences between and among the areas or regions of the brain

E | Electro-Chemical Cellular Functions
That means differences in electrical and chemical activities in the brain

M | Morphology
That means size, quantity, shape of brain anatomy.

Overall size of the brain doesn't matter, but the amount of grey matter in certain regions found to be associated with intelligence does make a difference. The areas of the brain that have been found to be connected to intelligence are in multiple regions of the brain, not in one single center.

O | Operations
That means neural efficiency and speed of connections in the brain.

Brain imaging shows that gifted brains are less active but more efficient. That is, at first glance on an MRI scan, it might appear that the brains of individuals with high intelligence are not doing much, but in reality what is happening is that their brains are working more efficiently.

R | Real Estate
That means the differences between and among the areas or regions of the brain.

The cortex layer in the brains of bright individuals starts out much thinner at an early age and then is at the thickest much later. After reaching the thickest condition, the maturation process (i.e. thinning & pruning) of the cortex takes place at a much more rapid pace in bright individuals.

What does this mean for parents and teachers of bright individuals? Think about this. The pre-frontal cortex controls organization. Might this explain why some of our bright middle-school aged children can do algebra but can't find the homework they know they did the night before?

E | Electro-Chemical Cellular Functions
That means differences in electrical and chemical activities in the brain.

Cortical Event Related Potential (ERP) is a way to use electrodes connected to the scalp to measure electrical current. Electrical activity is an indicator for efficient and effective cognitive processing and provides information into the working memory (an important process for reasoning and the guidance of decision making and behavior) and fluid intelligence (being able to think and reason abstractly and solve problems).

Appendix B
Gifted Characteristics and Resulting Behaviors

Gifted characteristics can manifest themselves in many ways. I remember when I first saw the "Gifted Characteristics and Concomitant Problems" chart in my gifted coursework. A characteristic was first listed and then the positive and the negative resulting behaviors were indicated. As I gained experience in working with gifted, I decided those terms should be changed. Those behaviors were more like signals for me as the teacher to insert supports for recognizing what was happening and making a plan to address the student's needs.

The following pages contain characteristics and associated possible behaviors. It is important to remember that not all gifted individuals display all of the characteristics typically listed in the literature that teachers and parents read regarding the needs of this population. Likewise, no matter the resulting behavior, it tells us what the child needs to be successful.

Gifted Characteristic
Gifted individuals retain a quantity of information and communicate using advanced vocabulary.
You Might See...
Gifted individuals have a ready recall of information - and responses to discussions about that information. Their responses are often detailed and very informative.
Or You Might See...
Gifted individuals can easily become so enthused with a discussion on a topic of which they are passionate or an expert, they can monopolize the conversation.

Gifted Characteristic
Gifted individuals are likely to have a highly developed sense of humor.
You Might See...
To make someone else chuckle or smile is one of the most selfless gifts we can offer another human being. Gifted individuals often excel at seeing the humorous side of a situation-even where others may not.
Or You Might See...
Sees opportunities abounding for a humorous commentary - and it can be at the expense of others they actually do care about deeply.

Gifted Characteristic
Gifted individuals are often perfectionists.
You Might See...
This is one characteristic that is highly praised in and rewarded by our society. Many of the highest paying jobs-traffic controllers, CFOs, surgeons, etc.-require utter perfection. They thrive on the nuances of projects, enjoy manipulating and working the details, composing, revising, and double and triple checking the end result against their high expectations. For many teachers, they are the dream student.
Or You Might See...
This characteristic can be an extreme source of stress as the child perfects the details of almost everything. If the perfectionism is strong enough, the child may never even really get started on the project because he fears his own expectations of the finished project could never be fully realized anyhow.

Gifted Characteristic

Gifted individuals evaluate and hold others to a high standard.

You Might See...

Where they may hold themselves to high personal standards, they also typically do so of others. When we hold others to a high standard, they tend to rise to that level. Classroom teachers know this, as do bosses and nearly anyone involved in human resources in private industry.

Or You Might See...

And then, of course, there is the group project. Typically, there is always at least one "slacker" in the group. There may also be at least one member who is less than enthused and concerned about the final product than the gifted individual. Scoping out the group project terrain, the gifted individual can either rebel against the group and demand to be allowed to do the project alone, or quietly take the final group efforts home and revise the entire thing to meet a higher quality expectation. Sometimes the group members love this and sometimes they don't.

Gifted Characteristic

Gifted individuals are concerned about ethics and the current events of the world around them.

You Might See...

It's not hard to see this at a young age. A routine drive to school with a gifted child can easily turn into a discussion of the moral issues surrounding the events overheard on the evening news broadcast. Being able to see the nuances of morality and to see someone else's perspectives, is a wonderful characteristic that results in empathetic and responsive citizens.

Or You Might See...

Gifted individuals want to have immediate solutions to the moral issues but cannot solve the wrong that they want to right. The gifted may be easily frustrated when classroom rules are not explained thoroughly or if the rationale for those rules is a tad flimsy.

Gifted Characteristic
Gifted individuals are curious and have a variety of interests.
You Might See...
When an individual is curious and has a variety of interests, they ask many questions and get excited about new ideas. When a person is found who can answer the questions at the level asked, new relationships are forged that are often lifelong connections.
Or You Might See...
If a person is not found who can answer the questions at the level asked, it can result in the curious individual going off on a tangent and not following through with their interests.

Gifted Characteristic
Gifted individuals are often very goal oriented.
You Might See...
Gifted individuals who are extremely goal oriented can be counted on to accomplish their goals.
Or You Might See...
When gifted individuals do not have control over their work schedule, they can be viewed as stubborn and inflexible when they want to accomplish the task differently.

Gifted Characteristic
Gifted individuals have the ability to concentrate and persist.
You Might See...
When given the "go ahead" to start a task, gifted individuals are often able to focus on a task and learn in depth.
Or You Might See...
Gifted individuals who are focusing and learning in-depth concepts really resist interruption.

Gifted Characteristic
Gifted individuals are often self-confident and like to be in leadership roles.
You Might See...
Those who like to be in leadership roles often find they have success influencing others.
Or You Might See...
Sometimes those who are gifted leaders and also very passionate about issues can be perceived as being very bossy.

Gifted Characteristic
Gifted individuals often enjoy and excel at an accelerated pace of learning.
You Might See...
When learning can be achieved at an accelerated pace, it does not take as long to master content.
Or You Might See...
When learning can be achieved at an accelerated pace, gifted individuals can be frustrated when the pace is not fast enough.

Gifted Characteristic
Gifted individuals often seek order when there is chaos.
You Might See...
Those who like to seek order often like to plan ahead and keep everything moving along.
Or You Might See...
Those who like to seek order and plan ahead do not do well with spontaneity. They do not react well to surprises of any kind.

Gifted Characteristic
Gifted individuals are typically very alert and observant.
You Might See…
When gifted individuals are very alert and observant, they can recognize both existing and possible problems quickly.
Or You Might See…
Those who are very alert and observant do not miss much that is going on and can state corrections in a less than polite manner.

Gifted Characteristic
Gifted individuals can be very much just that - individualistic.
You Might See…
Gifted individuals who are individualistic have a good sense that they are unique. They assert themselves and their ideas with confidence.
Or You Might See…
Those individualistic individuals can assert themselves forcefully and become aggressive as they challenge authority.

Gifted Characteristic
Gifted individuals are often avid readers.
You Might See…
Gifted individuals who are avid readers often have many books in process at the same time and finish books at a rapid rate.
Or You Might See…
Gifted individuals who are avid readers often have difficulty putting down the book and find it really easy to neglect other responsibilities.

Reference List

Education Week . Every Student Succeeds Act: December, 2017 Updates. Retrieved from: https://www.edweek.org/ topics/every-student-succeeds-act/index.html

Gottfredson, L.S. (2003). The science and politics of intelligence in gifted education. In Colangelo & Davis (Eds.). Handbook of gifted education, 24-40, Boston, MA: Pearson Education.

National Association for Gifted Children. Jacob Javits Gifted and Talented Students Education Act. Retrieved from: https://www.nagc.org/resources-publications/resources-university-professionals/ jacob-javits-gifted-talented-students

US Department of Education. PL 94-142: Progress in Education Children with Disabilities through IDEA. Retrieved from: https://www2.ed.gov/about/offices/list/osers/idea35/ history/index_pg10.html

Neuroscience for Kids has been created for all students and teachers who would like to learn about the nervous system. www.faculty.washington.edu/chudler/neurok. html

Brainworks TV Join UW bioengineering professor and BrainWorks host, Eric Chudler, as he takes viewers on a journey inside the human brain. With the goal of educating children about the wonders of neuroscience, this entertaining and informative episode discusses the benefits of exercise on the brain and learning. www. uwtv.org/series/brainworks

BrainGames online games sorted by suggested grade level ranges. www.faculty.washington.edu/chudler/chgames. html

Developing the Gifted Series
Order at www.fishtailpublishing.org

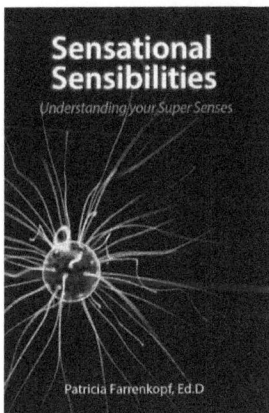

Volume 1
Sensational Sensibilities
Card deck available for purchase

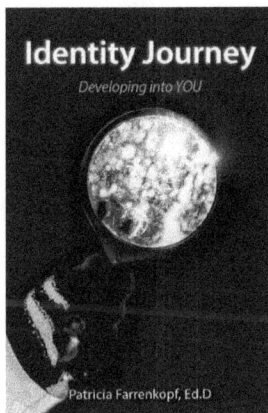

Volume 2
Identity Journey
Card deck and activity sheet
available for purchase

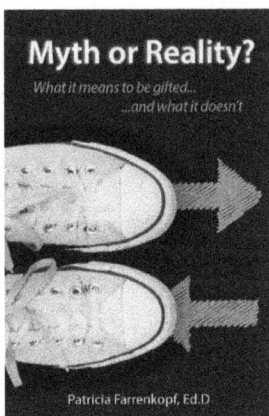

Volume 3
Myth or Reality?
Card deck available for purchase

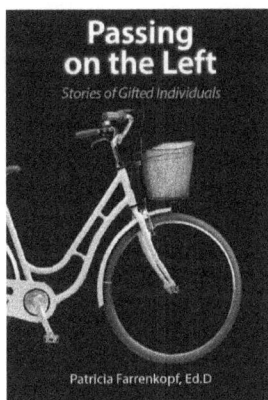

Volume 4
Passing on the Left
Card deck and activity sheet
available for purchase

Fishtail Publishing

9781733338059